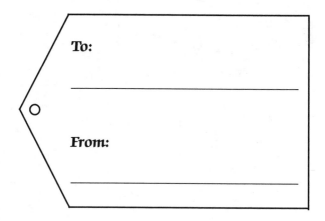

To:

_____

From:

_____

The Gift of Christmas

The Gift of

# Christmas

by Jim Gallery

B
B
Brighton Books
Nashville, TN

ISBN 1-58334-120-X

*The quoted ideas expressed in this book (but not scripture verses) are not, in all cases, exact quotations, as some have been edited for clarity and brevity. In all cases, the author has attempted to maintain the speaker's original intent. In some cases, quoted material for this book was obtained from secondary sources, primarily print media. While every effort was made to ensure the accuracy of these sources, the accuracy cannot be guaranteed. For additions, deletions, corrections or clarifications in future editions of this text, please write BRIGHTON BOOKS.*

All scripture quotations, unless otherwise indicated, are taken from the HOLY BIBLE, NEW INTERNATIONAL VERSION ©. NIV ©. Copyright © 1973, 1978, 1984, by International Bible Society. Used by permission of Zondervan Publishing House. All rights reserved.

Scripture taken from *THE MESSAGE.* Copyright © 1993, 1994, 1995, 1996. Used by permission of NavPress Publishing Group.

Scripture taken from the NEW AMERICAN STANDARD BIBLE®, Copyright © 1960, 1962, 1963, 1968, 1971, 1972, 1973, 1975, 1977, 1995 by The Lockman Foundation. Used by permission.

Printed in the United States of America
Cover Design & Page Layout: *Bart Dawson*

1 2 3 4 5 6 7 8 9 10 • 01 02 03 04 05 06 07 08 09 10

Acknowledgments: The author is indebted to Criswell Freeman for his support and friendship. A big thanks to Eloise Gallery for her editing help. The help of the wonderful staff at Walnut Grove Press has made the writing of this book a pleasurable experience.

Dedicated to
Ross White,
who lives every day
like it's Christmas

# Table of Contents

# Introduction

Charles Dickens, in describing a reformed Ebenezer Scrooge, wrote, "It was always said of him, that he knew how to keep Christmas well, if any man alive possessed the knowledge. May that be truly said of us, and all of us! And so, as Tiny Tim observed, 'God Bless Us, Every One!'"

This book has been written for all who seek to "keep Christmas well." If we are to do so, we must always be mindful of the true meaning of Christmas. Unfortunately, the true meaning of the season is easily obscured.

We live in a world full of distractions and busyness, a world that oftentimes hides the important and the meaningful behind the trite and the insignificant. And so it is with Christmas: The glory of the Christ child is the cornerstone of the season, yet Christ is too often left out of holiday celebrations.

Christmas can and should be a time for remembering God's great gift to mankind: His son Jesus Christ, a gift that brings meaning, significance, and salvation to the world. If we worship God and give thanks to Him, we find the true meaning of Christmas, but if we allow ourselves to become trapped in the snare of commercialization, we inevitably forfeit the peace and joy that God offers each of us.

On the pages that follow, you will find scripture, stories, prayers, quotations, sayings, and ideas for celebrating Christmas. May these words help you "keep Christmas well" by keeping its namesake, Christ Jesus, abiding in your heart.

Merry
Christmas

# Chapter 1

# God's Gift of Love

---

"For God so loved the world, that he
gave his only begotten Son, that
whosoever believeth in him should not
perish, but have everlasting life."

*John 3:16 KJV*

---

"…Joseph also went up from the town of Nazareth
in Galilee to Judea, to Bethlehem the town
of David, because he belonged to the house
and line of David. He went there to register
with Mary, who was pledged to be married
to him and was expecting a child. While they
were there, the time came for the baby
to be born, and she gave birth to her firstborn,
a son. She wrapped him in cloths, and laid him in a
manger, because there was no room
for them in the inn."

—————————————————————————— *Luke 2:4-7*

The birth of Jesus is a story about the fulfillment of prophecy. It is a story of the trust of a young woman, Mary, and the commitment of her fiancé, Joseph. It is a story of one glorious night that forever changed the world, a night when the sky was filled with an angelic choir singing to lowly shepherds as they watched their sheep, a night when noble Magi bowed their heads to a child named Jesus.

The birth of Jesus is also a love story: the story of God's love for the world. God loved His creation so much that He was willing to send His Son to live among men and to die for them. Jesus not only showed the way to salvation, he became the instrument of salvation. And thus, God's perfect love for mankind was made manifest.

God became a man: That is the Incarnation and that is the meaning of Christmas. God desires that all people accept His gift of love, but, for some, the mystery of the Incarnation is difficult to accept because it is difficult to understand. Louis Cassels, in his book *Christian Primer*, writes of one such man whose Christmas Eve experience unraveled the mystery.

*Cassels tells of a man who lived in a small farming community. The man did not believe in the Christmas story. He thought the whole idea strange and illogical. But one wintery night, birds and church bells changed the man's life forever.*

*On a snowy Christmas Eve, this man observed birds thumping into his window apparently seeking refuge from the winter storm. He felt compassion for the birds and decided to help.*

*The man knew his barn would be a safe refuge for his cold, feathered friends, but enlisting the birds' cooperation became quite a challenge. With the barn doors wide open and lights burning, he first tried to lead the birds to safety. No luck. Then, he tried shooing them toward the door. Still, no luck. Finally, he placed breadcrumbs along the path to the barn, but the birds still refused to cooperate. He thought, "If only I could become a bird, even for a little while, I could lead these lost creatures to safety."*

*At that very moment the church bells rang...and the man understood. He knew why God came to earth, and he understood the truth of the Christmas story. God became man so that He might lead us to salvation.*

---

Everyone must choose to accept God's gift of love...or not. The choice is easier for some than for others. But one truth remains sure—"For God so loved the world, that He gave His only begotten son...."

"Good news from heaven the angels bring,
Glad tidings to the earth they sing:
To us this day a child is given,
To crown us with the joy of heaven."

*Martin Luther*

"Jesus Christ was born into this world, not from it."
*Oswald Chambers*

"In the beginning was the Word, and the Word
was with God, and the Word was God.
He was with God in the beginning...The Word
became flesh and made his dwelling among us."

*John 1:1,14*

"The grace of God is infinite and eternal.
As it had no beginning, so it can have no end,
and being an attribute of God,
it is as boundless as infinitude."

*A. W. Tozer*

"When God's son took on flesh, He truly and
bodily took on, out of pure grace, our being,
our nature, ourselves. This was the eternal counsel
of the triune God. Now we are in Him....
We belong to Him because
we are in Him."

*Dietrich Bonhoeffer*

"The springs of love are in God, not in us."

*Oswald Chambers*

"The love of God is one of the great realities of
the universe, a pillar upon which the hope of
the world rests. But it is a personal, intimate thing
too. God does not love populations. He loves
people. He loves not masses, but men."

*A. W. Tozer*

"...I am the way and the truth and the life. No one comes to the Father except through me."

*Jesus*
*(John 14:6)*

"For to us a child is born, to us a son is given, and the government will be on his shoulders. And he will be called Wonderful Counselor, Mighty God, Everlasting Father, Prince of Peace."

*Isaiah 9:6*

"Christ alone can bring lasting peace —
peace with God —
peace among men and nations —
and peace within our hearts."

*Billy Graham*

"The peace that Jesus gives is never engineered
by circumstances on the outside."

*Oswald Chambers*

"And the peace of God, which transcends all
understanding, will guard your hearts and
your minds in Christ Jesus."

*Paul*
*(Philippians 4:7)*

"Joy to the World,
the Lord is come!
Let earth receive
her King..."

*Isaac Watts, 1719*

"A life of intimacy with God is characterized
by joy."

*Oswald Chambers*

"Joy is the serious business of heaven."

*C. S. Lewis*

"...Do not be afraid. I bring you good news
of great joy that will be for all people."

*Luke 2:10*

"God's love never ceases. Never... Our faith does not earn it anymore than our stupidity jeopardizes it. God doesn't love us less if we fail or more if we succeed. God's love never ceases.

*Max Lucado*

"How great is the love the Father has lavished on us, that we should be called children of God!"

*1 John 3:1*

Lord, thank you
for the greatest gift
ever given: Your Son.
Despite the busyness of
this day, remind me, Lord,
of the reason for this season.
Fill me with Your love and
help me always to reflect
that love to those whom You
place along my path.

*Amen*

Merry
Christmas

# Chapter 2

# Your Gift to God

---

"When they [the Magi] saw the star,
they were overjoyed. On coming to the
house, they saw the child with his
mother Mary and they bowed down and
worshiped him. Then they opened their
treasures and presented him with gifts
of gold and of incense and myrrh."

*Matthew 2:10-12*

---

The Christmas season provides each of us with special opportunities to praise the Giver of all things good. God has gifted us with His son, and we, in turn, are called upon to worship Him and share His good news. We praise God by word, by song, by deed, and by attitude.

On that first Christmas day, the Magi worshiped while the angels and shepherds praised and glorified God. The psalmist writes, "Come, let us bow down in worship…." (*Psalm 95:6*), and in the six short verses that comprise the 150th Psalm, he uses the word "praise" 13 times. David prays, "I will praise you, O Lord my God, with all my heart; I will glorify your name forever." (*Psalm 86:12*) As Christians, we should do no less.

*Many* families celebrate Advent, the coming of the Messiah. My niece, Sarah Beth Trinkle, shared with me how the observance of Advent has enhanced her family's worship at Christmas time.

The four Sundays before Christmas, Sara Beth and her family focus on four different characteristics that Jesus shared with his believers: joy, love, peace, and hope. Sarah Beth describes her family's celebration:

"We light a purple candle on the wreath each Sunday and share scripture and songs that remind us of what it means to be Christians at Christmas. Then, on Christmas Eve night, we light a white candle in the center of the wreath. This is the Christ candle, white for purity, and our family focuses on the great gift that God has given the world: His son Jesus. The wreath is circular and made of evergreen symbolizing the never-ending and constant love of Christ for us all."

Sarah Beth adds, "The best thing about Advent is knowing that for which we wait. Thankfully, we are no longer really waiting in the same way that people of ancient times did. We are no longer waiting for a savior because He has lived among us and risen from the dead. We have experienced the life and love that the one true God can give. When we celebrate Advent, we are joyfully reminded of the abundant life that was clothed in humanity and born to a frightened but trusting young couple so long ago."

"Come, let us bow down in worship,
let us kneel before the LORD
our Maker..."

*Psalm 95:6*

"Maintenance of the devotional mood is
indispensable to success in the Christian life."

*A.W. Tozer*

"The LORD is my strength and my song;
he has become my salvation.  He is my God,
and I will praise him, my father's God,
and I will exalt him."

*Exodus 15:2*

"Praise and thank God for who He is and
for what He has done for you."

*Billy Graham*

"Very early in the morning,
while it was still dark, Jesus got up,
left the house and went off
to a solitary place,
where he prayed."

*Mark 1:35*

"Whether we think of, or speak to, God,
   whether we act or suffer for him, all is prayer,
   when we have no other object than his love,
   and the desire of pleasing him."

*John Wesley*

"Let your mind soak in the deliverance of God."

*Oswald Chambers*

"Since, then, you have been raised with Christ,
   set your hearts on things above, where
   Christ is seated at the right hand of God.
   Set your minds on things above..."

*Colossians 3:1,2*

"Praise be to the God and Father of our Lord
Jesus Christ, who has blessed us in the heavenly
realms with every spiritual blessing in Christ.
For he chose us in him before the creation of the
world to be holy and blameless in his sight."

*Ephesians 1:3,4*


"Whenever the living creatures give glory, honor
and thanks to him who sits on the throne and
who lives for ever and ever, the twenty-four elders
fall down before him who sits on the throne,
and worship him who lives for ever and ever.
They lay their crowns before the throne and say:
"You are worthy, our Lord and God, to receive
glory and honor and power, for you created all
things, and by your will they were created
and have their being."

*Revelation 4:9-11*

"Intimacy may not be rushed....We can't dash
into God's presence and choke down spiritual
inwardness before we hurry to our
one o'clock appointment. Inwardness is
time-consuming, open only to minds willing
to sample spirituality in small bites,
savoring each one.

*Calvin Miller*

"This day's bustle and hurly-burly would too often
and too soon call us away from Jesus' feet.
These distractions must be immediately
dismissed, or we shall know only
the 'barrenness of busyness.'"

*A.W. Tozer*

"Be still, and know that I am God..."

*Psalm 46:10*

## <u>*Worship Ideas for Family and Friends...*</u>

❀ Read the Christmas story on Christmas Eve
    night.

❀ Attend a Christmas Eve worship service at a
    local church.

❀ Bake a white birthday cake for Jesus on
    Christmas Eve.

❀ Make a Nativity with your children and explain
    to them the significance of each part.

❀ Leave only the Christmas lights on and listen to
    great hymns and carols.

❀ Give all gifts on Christmas Eve and spend
    Christmas Day honoring Jesus.

❀ Collect nativity scenes and bring them out each
    year. Remember Christmas's past and how
    God has blessed over the years.

*L*ord, just as the angels
glorified You, just as the shepherds
were filled with praise, and just as the
Magi worshipped You, may I also
bow my head and lift my heart to You.
Lord, You gave Your best for me.
May my sacrifice of worship be
acceptable in your sight on this
day and every day.

*Amen*

Merry
Christmas

# Chapter 3

# Your Gift to Family

---

"When Joseph and Mary had done
everything required by the Law of
the Lord, they returned to Galilee to
their own town of Nazareth. And the
child grew and became strong; he was
filled with wisdom, and the grace of
God was upon him."

*Luke 2:39,40*

---

In His infinite wisdom and with a power that passes all understanding, God, when He created man and woman, did something more: He created the family. God knew the important role that the family would play in the lives of His children. Our families provide love, support, a sense of belonging, and encouragement. Just as Joseph and Mary provided a family in which Jesus might grow in strength and wisdom, we, too, should provide the same for our loved ones.

Like no other holiday, Christmas brings families together to celebrate and share in the warmth of the season. During these special days, we should make certain our gifts, as well as our words and deeds, reflect the spirit of the One whose birth we celebrate.

Convincing a 6-year-old to spend Christmas Eve in the kitchen baking cookies with his family was not easy. My son, Jimmy, had more important things to do, namely playing with his toys and teasing his sister. Only with bribes of cookie dough, along with promises that he could lick the bowl, did Jimmy finally join the family cookie-baking project.

My daughter Julie and her mom were the real bakers in the family while Jimmy and I offered suggestions, provided the correct utensils, and selected the Christmas music. Most importantly, we tested the cookie dough early and often. The old familiar carols, the aroma of freshly-baked cookies, and the smiles on all our faces pointed to the inescapable fact…it was Christmas.

This day was special, and the cookies were for very special people. After we finished preparing the goodies, we joined in wrapping the sweets in brightly-colored Christmas paper. After topping our packages with bows and ribbons, we took our gifts and climbed into the car.

Our first stop was the fire station where we met special people who couldn't be with their families on Christmas Eve. Their "thank you's" were genuine, and my children were duely impressed by the fire engines. The next stop was the emergency room at our local hospital. The receptionist accepted our gift with thanks. Then, we were off to our final destination: the police department. The city's finest were appreciative.

On this particular Christmas Eve, our family gave back to our community in a small way, but we gave something much greater to ourselves. As a family, we were reminded of the joy of giving.

The Christmas season is a time to celebrate God's gift of His Son, a gift that He freely gave to all the world. When we serve others with our gifts and possessions, we can make the God-honoring statement Joshua made, "...as for me and my house, we will serve the Lord." (Joshua 24:15, NASB)

"Homes that are built on anything other than love
are bound to crumble."

*Billy Graham*

"Love is extravagant in the price it is willing to
pay, the time it is willing to give, the hardships it is
willing to endure, and the strength it is willing to
spend. Love never thinks in terms of 'how little,'
but always in terms of 'how much.' Love gives,
love knows, and love lasts."

*Joni Eareckson Tada*

"Therefore everyone who hears these words of mine and puts them into practice is like a wise man who built his house on the rock. The rain came down, the streams rose, and the winds blew and beat against that house; yet it did not fall, because it had its foundation on the rock."

Jesus
*Matthew 7:24,25*

"Have your heart right with Christ,
and he will visit you often, and so turn weekdays
into Sundays, meals into sacraments, homes
into temples, and earth into heaven."

*C. H. Spurgeon*

"No other structure can replace the family.
Without it, our children have no moral
foundation. Without it, they become moral
illiterates whose only law is self."

*Chuck Colson*

"We must strengthen our commitment to model
strong families ourselves, to live by godly
priorities in a culture where self so often
supersedes commitment to others. And
as we not only model but assertively reach out
to help others, we must realize that even
huge societal problems are solved
one person at a time."

*Chuck Colson*

"There is a time for risky love. There is a time for extravagant gestures. There is a time to pour out your affections on one you love. And when the time comes, seize it, don't miss it.

*Max Lucado*

"It is a reverent thing to see an ancient castle or building not in decay, or to see a fair timber tree sound and perfect. How much more to behold an ancient and noble family that has stood against the waves and weathers of time."

*Francis Bacon*

"Husbands, love your wives, just as Christ loved
the church and gave himself up for her."

*Ephesians 5:25*

"...the wife must respect her husband..."

*Ephesians 5:33*

"Children, obey your parents in the Lord, for
this is right. 'Honor your father and mother'—
which is the first commandment…"

*Ephesians 6:1,2*

"Fathers, do not exasperate your children;
instead, bring them up in the training and
instruction of the Lord…"

*Ephesians 6:4*

"Many have forgotten the value of characteristics
and activities which identify the family as unique
and different. They are called 'traditions.'"

*James Dobson*

"Hear, O Israel: The LORD our God, the LORD
is one. Love the LORD your God with all your
heart and with all your soul and with all your
strength. These commandments that I give
you today are to be upon your hearts. Impress
them on your children. Talk about them when
you sit at home and when you walk along
the road, when you lie down and when you
get up. Tie them as symbols on your hands
and bind them on your foreheads. Write them
on the doorframes of your houses and
on your gates."

*Deuteronomy 6:4-9*

"The Christian is supposed to love his neighbor,
and since his wife is his nearest neighbor,
she should be his deepest love."

*Martin Luther*

"Even if marriages are made in heaven,
man has to be responsible
for the maintenance."

*James Dobson*

"Her children arise and call her blessed;
 her husband also, and he praises her…"

*Proverbs 31:28*


"Train up a child in the way he should go:
 and when he is old,
 he will not depart from it."

*Proverbs 22:6 KJV*

"When home is ruled according to God's Word,
angels might be asked to stay with us,
and they would not find themselves
out of their element."

*Charles Spurgeon*

"Don't urge me to leave you or to turn back
from you. Where you go I will go, and where you
stay I will stay. Your people will be my people
and your God my God. Where you die I will die,
and there I will be buried. May the LORD
deal with me, be it ever so severely, if
anything but death separates you and me."

*Ruth to her mother-in-law Naomi*
*(Ruth 1:16,17)*

## Ideas For Celebrating With the Family

❋ Write a Christmas play involving the whole family and videotape it.

❋ Gather the family together and view videos of Christmases past.

❋ Arrange with family members, near and far away, to light a candle at the same time on Christmas eve in honor of Christ and your family.

❋ Light a candle in memory of a family member.

❋ Tell family Christmas stories on Christmas Eve.

❋ Leave love notes all around the home for your spouse.

❋ Enjoy an evening searching the community for the best Christmas lights.

*L*ord, thank you for
the gift of my family. Always help
me to be grateful for that gift,
and help me to demonstrate my
gratitude through actions as
well as words. During this
Christmas season, Lord, help me
to be a loving example of
Your boundless love
and infinite grace.

*Amen*

Merry
Christmas

# Chapter 4

# Your Gift to Friends

---

"Greater love has no one than this,
that he lay down his life
for his friends."

*John 15:13*

---

Beautiful cards arrive at Christmastime, many of which contain warm notes; a few even hold painstakingly crafted summaries of the senders' "doings" for the year gone by. As the holidays approach, friends take time to call each other and to exchange photographs. Christmas parties provide opportunities to reconnect with old friends and make new ones. Everywhere we turn, it seems, Christmas festivities remind us of the importance of friendship.

Jesus is both friend and savior to mankind. His willingness to die on our behalf is the greatest expression of love that one friend can show to another. As believers, we owe Him a debt that we can never fully repay. Thus, on this Christmas, and every Christmas, we renew our friendships here on earth all the while giving praise and thanksgiving for the birth and the life of the heavenly friend who was born to die for us.

*E*ach year after Thanksgiving, Bonnie DeArmond and her family planned their annual Christmas "Ring and Run" celebration. First, the DeArmonds gathered together and began making a large assortment of home-made gifts. Then, when presents filled the dining room table to overflowing, each family member chose friends who would be the recipients of these gifts.

*Then the fun began.*

On one special evening, the normally mild-mannered DeArmonds carried out a covert operation. With gifts in hand, they climbed into their family van. As they approached the targeted home, the van lights went dark and the side door quietly opened to let Sterling, Meagan, or Schaeffer sneak to the house. A gift was placed at the front door, the bell was rung, and the child raced back to the waiting van. Ring and run. Bonnie and family were far down the road before the friends discovered their gifts.

After completing the drop-offs, the DeArmonds returned home to await the inevitable calls from delighted friends. Bonnie and her family made Christmas memories as they shared the gift of friendship.

"Two things upon this changing earth
can neither change nor end;
the splendor of Christ's humble birth,
the love of friend for friend."

*Anonymous*

"Friends are an indispensable part of a meaningful life. They are the ones who share our burdens and multiply our blessings.

*Beverly LaHaye*


"It is the duty of every Christian to be Christ to his neighbor."

*Martin Luther*


"Friendship is something that raised us almost above humanity.... It is the sort of love one can imagine between angels.

*C. S. Lewis*

"...love your neighbor as yourself."

Jesus
(Matthew 19:19)

"And who is my neighbor? In reply Jesus said,
'A man was going down from Jerusalem to
Jericho, when he fell into the hands of robbers.
They stripped him of his clothes, beat him and
went away, leaving him half dead. A priest
happened to be going down the same road, and
when he saw the man, he passed by on the other
side. So too, a Levite, when he came to the place
and saw him, passed by on the other side. But a
Samaritan, as he traveled, came where the man
was; and when he saw him, he took pity on him.
He went to him and bandaged his wounds, pouring
on oil and wine. Then he put the man on his own
donkey, took him to an inn and took care of him.
The next day he took out two silver coins and gave
them to the innkeeper. 'Look after him,' he said,
'and when I return, I will reimburse you for any
extra expense you may have.'"

*Luke 10:29-35*

"What a friend we have in Jesus."

*Old Saying*

"A friend loves at all times…"

*Proverbs 17:17*

"Do not forsake your friend…"

*Proverbs 27:10*

"When you received Jesus Christ as
your personal Lord and Savior,
you began a relationship
not only with Him but also with
all other Christians."

*Billy Graham*

"Friends are angels who lift our feet when
our weary wings have trouble remembering
how to fly."

*Anonymous*

"By this all men will know that you are my disciples, if you love one another."

*John 13:35*

"Be united with other Christians.
A wall with loose bricks is not good.
The bricks must be cemented together."

*Corrie ten Boom*

"God has given us two hands: one for receiving
and the other for giving."

*Billy Graham*

"May the God who gives endurance and encouragement give you a spirit of unity among yourselves as you follow Christ Jesus, so that with one heart and mouth you may glorify the God and Father of our Lord Jesus Christ."

*Romans 15:5*

"Friendship is one of the sweetest joys of life.
Many might have failed beneath the
bitterness of their trial had they
not found a friend."

*C. H. Spurgeon*

"No receipt opens the heart but a true friend,
to whom you may impart griefs, joys, fears,
hopes, suspicions, counsels, and
whatever lies upon the heart."

*Francis Bacon*

"The worst solitude is to be destitute of
sincere friendship."

*Francis Bacon*

"The dearest friend on earth is a mere shadow
compared with Jesus Christ."

*Oswald Chambers*

"...I have called you friends, for everything that
I learned from my Father I have made
known to you."

*Jesus*
*(John 15:15)*

"If one falls down, his friend can help him up.
But pity the man who falls and has
no one to help him up!"

*Ecclesiastes 4:10*

"A friend is one who makes me do my best."

*Oswald Chambers*

"...there is a friend who sticks closer than
a brother."

*Proverbs 18:24*

"In friendship's fragrant garden
There are flowers of every hue.
Each with its own fair beauty,
And its gift of joy for you."

*Anonymous*

"It is more blessed to give than to receive."

*Acts 20:35 KJV*

"Do unto others as you would have them
do to you."

*Luke 6:31*

"What makes the Dead Sea dead?
Because it is all the time receiving, but
never giving out anything. Why is it that many
Christians are cold?  Because they are
all the time receiving, never giving out."

*D. L. Moody*

## <u>Celebrating Christmas with Friends</u>

❂ Have an open house for neighbors.

❂ Invite neighborhood children in to bake
    (and taste) cookies.

❂ Find a photograph of the last time you were
    together with your friend.  Frame it and
    send it to your friend with a letter of
    appreciation.

*L*ord, You have given me
so much. One of Your greatest
blessings is the blessing of friendship.
My friends love me and encourage
me…help me, Lord, to always love
and encourage them. And
let me use this season's celebration
of Christ's birth as a time to
strengthen my ties with the friends
and neighbors whom You place
along my path.

*Amen*

Merry
Christmas

# Chapter 5

# Your Gift to Community

---

"…my eyes have seen your salvation,
which you have prepared in the sight of
all people, a light for revelation to
the Gentiles and for glory to
your people Israel."

*Luke 2:30-32*

---

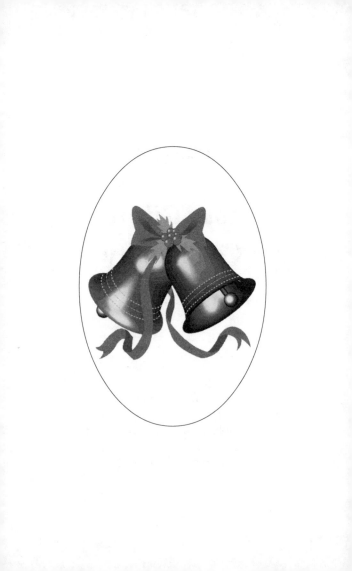

When Jesus was only eight days old, his parents took Him to the temple where they were met by a devout man named Simeon. God had promised Simeon that he would not die until he saw the Savior. Simeon held Jesus and praised God for His salvation for Israel and for *all people*.

The Christmas Gift of God is a gift to all people. Whether they live next door or across the ocean, God intends for people everywhere to accept His Gift of love and salvation. Just before Jesus ascended into heaven, He told His followers that they would be "my witnesses in Jerusalem, and in all Judea and Samaria, and to the ends of the earth." (*Acts 1:8*)

God does not restrict his gifts to the holiday season, and neither should we. As Christians we are commanded to share our possessions, our time, our compassion, and our witness with those in need. The celebration of Christ's birth should serve as a reminder that we must share our gifts on Christmas day *and* every other day of the year.

*I*t was Saturday afternoon, and the youth of our church were being youth. They were talking and laughing and all 50 boys and girls were trying to wedge themselves into a single van, while four other vehicles sat empty. The atmostphere was festive and slightly chaotic.

Every year our young people made a pilgrimage to the local shopping mall where they would find the perennial "Angel Tree." This tree was adorned not with ornaments, but with the names of children from families who could not afford Christmas gifts. Beside each child's name was a gift request.

After arriving at the mall, the youth divided themselves into small groups. Each group selected a name from the Angel Tree and then spent an hour shopping for their special child. The young people enjoyed themselves immensely, but more importantly, they helped meet a need in the life of one of God's children. The youth of our church also realized how blessed they were to have the necessities of life.

This annual trip to the mall was a tangible demonstration of compassion in action. Whenever we show compassion, we model the behavior of our Savior (Matthew 9:36). Each time we lend a hand or extend a simple kindness to a neighbor in need, we become just a little more like Jesus.

"Do all the good you can.
By all the means you can.
In all the ways you can.
In all the places you can.
At all the times you can.
To all the people you can.
As long as ever you can."

*John Wesley*

"We hurt people by being too busy.
　　　　Too busy to notice their needs."

*Billy Graham*

"For I was hungry and you gave me something
to eat, I was thirsty and you gave me
something to drink, I was a stranger and you
invited me in, I needed clothes and you clothed
me, I was sick and you looked after me, I was in
prison and you came to visit me. Then the
righteous will answer him 'Lord, when did we see
you hungry and feed you, or thirsty and give you
something to drink? When did we see you a
stranger and invite you in, or needing clothes and
clothe you? When did we see you sick or in prison
and go to visit you?' The King will reply, 'I tell you
the truth, whatever you did for one of the least of
these brothers of mine, you did for me.'"

*Matthew 25:34-40*

"Make it a rule, and pray to God to help you
to keep it, never, if possible, to lie down at
night without being able to say: 'I have made
one human being at least a little wiser, or a
little happier, or at least a little better this day.'"

*Charles Kingsley*

"And if anyone gives even a cup of cold water
to one of these little ones because he is my
disciple, I tell you the truth, he will certainly not
lose his reward."

*Jesus*
*(Matthew 10:42)*

"Give away your life; you'll find life given back,
but not merely given back, given back with bonus
and blessing. Giving, not getting, is the way.
Generosity begets generosity."

*Luke 6:38 (The Message)*

"Lonely people, hurting people need someone to
help them up. To encourage them, to let them
know they're not alone. Who are the helpers, the
comforters for the times when we're bleeding and
need a transfusion of love?"

*Billy Graham*

"If doing a good act in public will excite others to
do more good, then ...
Let your Light shine to all ..."

*John Wesley*

"Miss no opportunity to do good."

*John Wesley*

"…let your light shine before men,
that they may see your good deeds and
praise your Father in heaven."

*Matthew 5:16*

"We must focus on prayer as the main thrust
to accomplish God's will and purpose on earth.
The forces against us have never been
greater, and this is the only way we can release
God's power to become victorious."

*John Maxwell*

"How many people have you made homesick
for God?"

*Oswald Chambers*

"Taking the gospel to people wherever they are —
death row, the ghetto, or next door
is frontline evangelism. Frontline love.
It is our one hope for breaking down barriers
and for restoring the sense of community,
of caring for one another, that our decadent,
impersonalized culture has sucked out of us."

*Chuck Colson*

"God of our life, there are days when the burdens
we carry chafe our shoulders and weigh us
down; when the road seems dreary and endless,
the skies grey and threatening; when our lives
have no music in them, and our hearts are
lonely, and our souls have lost their courage.
Flood the path with light, run our eyes to
where the skies are full of promise; tune
our hearts to brave music; give us the sense of
comradeship with heroes and saints of every age;
and so quicken our spirits that we may be able to
encourage the souls of all who journey with us on
the road of life, to Your honour and glory."

*St. Augustine*

"God grant we may not hinder those who are
battling their way slowly into the light."

*Oswald Chambers*

"Every time we encourage someone we give them a transfusion of courage."

*Chuck Swindoll*

"May happiness touch your life today as warmly as you have touched the lives of others."

*Old Saying*

"He climbs highest who helps another up."

*Zig Ziglar*

"Give us, O God, the vision which can see Your love in the world in spite of human failure.
Give us the faith to trust Your goodness in spite of our ignorance and weakness.
Give us the knowledge that we may continue to pray with understanding hearts.
And show us what each one of us can do to set forward the coming of the day of universal peace."

*Frank Borman*
*Christmas Eve Prayer*
*Apollo 8 Space Mission,*
*1968*

## Ideas for Building Community at Christmastime

❀ Visit a nursing home. Bring children, cards, and cookies.

❀ Enlist your Sunday School class and go caroling door-to-door.

❀ Volunteer to help a local charity and take your children or grandchildren along to help.

❀ Give to world-wide missions.

*L*ord, I am so blessed, but
sometimes, I take my blessings
for granted. You have given to me
far beyond anything I deserved or
imagined. You have blessed me that I
might be a blessing to others. Help me,
Lord, always to remember the glorious
gifts You have given me, and help me
to do Your will by giving generously
of my time and possessions to
those in need.

*Amen*

# Chapter 6

# God's Gift of Life

---

"Jesus said to her, 'I am the
resurrection and the life. He
who believes in me will live, even
though he dies; and whoever lives
and believes in me will never die.
Do you believe this?'"

*John 11:25,26*

---

When we accept God's gift of love, we also receive God's gift of life. As the pages on the calendar turn, the celebration of Christmas soon gives way to the celebration of Easter. The cradle leads to the cross. But no grave can hold God's gift of love, and Jesus lives that we might live.

Jesus tells us, "...I have come that they might have life, and have it to the full." (*John 10:10b*) God has great plans for His children; He gives us the gift of life so that we might rise above our circumstances and rise above the trials and tribulations of this earthly existence. God does not intend that we "just get by" nor does He intend that we do the best we can *under* the circumstances...He wants us to rise *above* them.

When Jesus overcame death, He overcame the world, (*John 16:33*) and He desires that all of His followers live victoriously. When we celebrate the birthday of Jesus, we must also remember the reason He came into this world: He is the "resurrection and the life."

*T*o "do Christmas well," we must see beyond the cradle to the cross. Jesus left His home in heaven and subjected Himself to the limitations of man for a reason. He was born to die. God's plan of salvation came through the event of the Incarnation.

I remember the day Lauryn Moody cried. At our weekly Bible study, we were discussing the death and resurrection of Jesus. As the discussion progressed, tears welled up in Lauryn's eyes. Tears flowed as she reflected on God's ultimate sacrifice for mankind…and for Lauryn Moody. All of us in the group were deeply moved, and I renewed myself to a growing understanding of what God had done for me through the Passion of Jesus.

As we celebrate the birth of Christ, we celebrate His death and resurrection. Through His resurrection we have life abundant and life eternal. Max Lucado writes about the "One who gave up the crown of heaven for a crown of thorns." Lucado adds, "He did it for you. Just for you."

"Our salvation comes to us so easily
because it cost God so much."

Oswald Chambers

"I have a better Caretaker…. He it is who lies in a manger … but at the same time sits at the right hand of God, the almighty Father. Therefore be at rest."

*Martin Luther, in a letter to his wife Kate: 1546, eleven days before his death.*

"Where, O death, is your victory?
Where, O death, is your sting?
...But thanks be to God!
He gives us the victory through
our Lord Jesus Christ."

*I Corinthians 15:55,57*

"Let God have you, and let God love you--and
don't be surprised if your heart begins to hear
music you've never heard and your feet learn to
dance as never before."

*Max Lucado*

Always new.
Always exciting.
Always full of promise.
The mornings of our lives,
Each a personal daily miracle."

*Gloria Gaither*

"Christmas is about a baby,
born in a stable,
who changed the world forever."

*John Maxwell*

"Life in the presence of God should be known to us in conscious experience. It is a life to be enjoyed every moment of every day."

*A. W. Tozer*

"It is not what we do that matters, but what a sovereign God chooses to do through us. God doesn't want our success; He wants us."

*Chuck Colson*

"The manger is a symbol of what can happen when Jesus Christ resides inside us."

*Bill Hybels*

"As I quietly abide in You and let Your life flow
into me, what freedom it is to know that
the Father does not see my threadbare
patience or insufficient trust, rather only
Your patience, Lord, and Your confidence
that the Father has everything in hand.
In Your faith I thank You right now for a more
glorious answer to my prayer than I can imagine.
Amen."

*Catherine Marshall*

"The responsible person seeks to make his or her
whole life a response to the question and
call of God."

*Dietrich Bonhoeffer*

"So, chosen by God for this new life of love,
dress in the wardrobe God picked out for you:
compassion, kindness, humility,
quiet strength, discipline."

*Colossians 3:12 (The Message)*

"Our Lord has written the promise of the
resurrection, not in books alone,
but in every leaf in springtime."

*Martin Luther*

"Christ's work of making new men...
is not mere improvement,
but transformation."

*C. S. Lewis*

"What do you think God
wants you to do?
The answer is that He wants you
to turn to Jesus and open
your life to Him."

*Billy Graham*

"Here I am!
I stand at the door and knock.
If anyone hears my voice and
opens the door, I will come in and
eat with him, and he with me."

*Revelation 3:20*

"If we surrender our hearts to God we may expect
a wondrous enlargement."

*A. W. Tozer*

An infinite God can give all of Himself to each of
His children. He does not distribute Himself that
each may have a part, but to each one He gives all
of Himself as fully as if there were no others."

*A. W. Tozer*

"Abide in Jesus, the sinless one —
which means, give up all of self and
its life, and dwell in God's will and
rest in His strength. This is what brings the power
that does not commit sin."

*Andrew Murray*

"I am the vine; you are the branches,
If a man remains in me and I in him,
he will bear much fruit; apart from me
you can do nothing."

*Jesus*
(John 15:5)

*The Gift of Christmas*

"Therefore, if anyone is in Christ,
he is a new creation; the old has gone,
the new has come."

*2 Corinthians 5:17*


"Jesus Christ died on the Cross and rose from
the grave. He paid the penalty for our sin and
bridged the gap between God and people."

*Billy Graham*

"Because he lives I can face tomorrow.
Because he lives all fear is gone.
Because I know he holds the future,
and life is worth the living,
just because he lives."

*Bill and Gloria Gaither*

"The joy of anything, from a blade of grass
upwards, is to fulfill its created purpose."
*Oswald Chambers*

"I thank my God every time I remember you.
In all my prayers for all of you, I always
pray with joy because of your partnership
in the gospel from the first day until now,
being confident of this, that he who began a
good work in you will carry it on to completion
until the day of Christ Jesus."
*Philippians 1:3-6*

"The virgin will be with child and will give birth to a son, and they will call him Immanuel, which means, 'God with us.'"

*Matthew 1:23*

"If only we would stop lamenting and look up, God is here. Christ is risen. The Spirit has been poured out from on high."

*A. W. Tozer*

"We may run, walk, stumble, drive, or fly,
but let us never lose sight of the reason for
the journey, or miss a chance to see a
rainbow on the way."

*Gloria Gaither*

Lord, the celebration of
Jesus' birth is joyous. During this
time of thanksgiving, keep me ever
mindful of Christ's life and
His sacrifice. Lord, I know that
I can experience abundant life and
eternal life with You because of Your
Christmas Gift to the world.
Thank You.

*Amen*

*"Thanks be to God for his indescribable gift."*

2 Corinthians 9:15

# About the Author

Jim Gallery lives and writes in Middle Tennessee. He serves as publisher for both Brighton Books and Walnut Grove Press. In addition, Jim is a sought-after speaker and lecturer. He has over 20 year's experience as a pastor.

Jim is a graduate of the University of South Florida and the New Orleans Baptist Theological Seminary. He is the father of two children, Julie and Jimmy.

Some of his other titles include:

*God Can Handle It*
*God Can Handle It... Teenagers*
*God Can Handle It... Fathers*
*Prayers of a Godly Woman*
*Prayers of a Righteous Man*
*Prayers of a Dedicated Teacher*
*Teachers Change the World...*

Brighton
Books